T0129171

TODOS SANTOS
AND
BAJA BCS MEXICO

TODOS SANTOS

AND

BAJA BCS MEXICO

A TRAVEL GUIDE

JOHN P. CROSS

TODOS SANTOS AND BAJA BCS MEXICO
A Travel Guide

iUniverse books may be ordered through booksellers or by contacting:

iUniverse
1663 Liberty Drive
Bloomington, IN 47403
www.iuniverse.com
1-800-Authors (1-800-288-4677)

Because of the dynamic nature of the Internet, any web addresses or links contained in this book may have changed since publication and may no longer be valid. The views expressed in this work are solely those of the author and do not necessarily reflect the views of the publisher, and the publisher hereby disclaims any responsibility for them.

Accuracy. Time changes things. A business may move locations or go out of business. Information may change without notice. Be aware.

Any people depicted in stock imagery provided by Thinkstock are models, and such images are being used for illustrative purposes only. Certain stock imagery © Thinkstock.

ISBN: 978-1-5320-3028-4 (sc)
ISBN: 978-1-5320-2975-2 (e)

Library of Congress Control Number: 2017912089

Print information available on the last page.

iUniverse rev. date: 09/12/2017

Contents

"If you reject the food, ignore the customs, fear the religion, and avoid the people, you might better stay home."
-James Michener

Dedication

To My Mother, Father, and Sister.

"Travel is fatal to prejudice, bigotry, and narrow mindedness, and many of our people need it sorely on these accounts. Broad, wholesome, charitable views of man and things cannot be acquired by vegetating in one little corner of the earth all one's lifetime."

–Mark Twain.

JOHN P. CROSS

John currently lives in Atlanta, Georgia. The author has traveled completely around the world to all seven continents and Antarctica and the Arctic. Altogether, Cross has been to more than seventy countries. He has traveled the Trans-Siberian Railway from China and Mongolia to Moscow and St. Petersburg in Russia.

Cross has a BA in History from Troy University, and a MA in History from University of Alabama. Cross received his minors in Geography and Spanish. He is a former teacher and a publishing sales representative. Travel is his passion

Preface

"When you look like your passport photo, it
is time to go home."
                                    –Erma Bombeck

This book is about Todos Santos in Baja Sur Mexico
(BCS). I have visited Todos Santos on numerous occasions.
It is easy to "fall in love" with Todos Santos. In fact, I
plan to move there. Todos Santos is North of Cabo San
Lucas, It has a great climate, Near the Pacific Ocean and
mountains.

It is ideal for surfers, fisherman, artists and artisans
and writers. Baja California is mostly a desert ecosystem
surrounded by the Pacific Ocean on the west and Mar
de Cortez on the East. It is a peninsular separate from
the main land of Mexico. At first, many thought it was
an island.

This book is the accumulation of travel experiences
of the author in Mexico. The arm chair traveler, or
intrepid traveler may benefit from the travel experiences
of the author. I hope you find the book an inspiration
and motivation to "Just Go!". In the appendices you will
find a useful chapter on the economics and finance for

preparing your trip on a budget. Also, there is a chapter on using computer apps. To plan your trip.

There is a planning and packing guide. You will also find a mini Spanish travel dictionary with essential Spanish words and phrases to learn before you go to Mexico. I give you a list of hotels in various prices ranges. I do the same with restaurants. From budget class to moderate and expensive. You make your choice according to your budget. There is something for everyone. An option is to travel with a group where hotels and food are included. This is a good way to go whale watching. Group travel reduces the cost of the hotel and the use of the boat. The key is to do your research and planning. Otherwise contact your favorite travel agent.

The book also covers Baja South California, everything South of La Paz and Todos Santos. This includes Loreto, Los Barriles, Cabo Jose, the corridor, and the ever popular Cabo San Lucas. Attention is given to ecotourism. Coverage is given to whale watching and release of ocean turtles. Because the oceans are the largest ecosystems on earth. We only have one planet and we must take care of the environment. This is of vital interest to human kind. The book will not disappoint. I included personal experiences, stories, history, and culture. I love my many trips to Mexico beginning in 1969. It is a country to easily enjoy and to love. I hope you enjoy Mexico as I have.

Adios, and Hasta Luego! Vaya con dios mi amigos!

Reviewer

Dr. Allen Jones, Chairman of History, Troy University writes "John Cross does an excellent job of integrating the history, and his many anecdotes, into the travel narrative. He has created a book that is easy, and interesting to read. I would definitely recommend this book."

Cross is also a frequent contributor to Travel Advisor as a reviewer. He is well traveled.

Happy travels! John P. Cross Atlanta, Georgia USA

"He who is outside his door already has the hardest part of his journey behind him."

-Dutch proverb

"I read. I travel. I become."

-Derek Wolcott

1

Todos Santos Baja: A brief history

"If you don't know history, then you don't know anything. You are a leaf that don't know it is part of a tree."
                                    –Michael Chrichton

In 1723, father Jaime Bravo founded the Jesuit mission in what was to become Todos Santos (all saints). Their purpose was to convert the Indians to the catholic religion. But there were clashes in culture and epidemics. Not all was cordial.

The mission became the Cathedral Pilar where you can see the statue of Virgin of Pilar. The Cathedral is next to the Hotel California and faces the town plaza where many festivals are held. The Cathedral is an excellent example of early California colonial religion. During the 19th century Todos Santos prospered as the sugar cane capital. Because of the lack of fresh water the sugar mills slowly closed. The last one closed in 1965.

The Mexican Revolution where Pancho Villa and Zapata fight for the common people lasted from 1910 to 1920. The war had its effects on all levels of society. Battles were fought in Todos Santos and Pescadero, Baja.

From Todos Santos the Mexican Revolution produced a hero and woman of valor. She made her place in history because of her exploits. Her name was La Coronella Maria de la Luz Espinosa Barrera. She actually received a pension as a veteran of the Mexican Revolution.

They called her La Coronella because she was born in Todos Santos in 1860 and she organized during the war an espionage group of woman. They served tequila to the opposite soldiers to get them to talk and reveal military plans. She often dressed like a man and wore a gun. It was said she could out drink, out smoke and out gamble a man. Even after the war she carried a pistol. She served mostly Zapata and she knew Villa. She was outstanding in her espionage, and as a courier. It is said she did hand to hand combat in the war.

The hotel California has a restaurant and bar named La Coronella in her behalf. It is simply called La Coronella. There is a painting of her in a dress. Some say her ghost appears on occasions in the hotel. Las Soldaderas Translated to English the word means women soldiers of the Mexican revolution.

La Coronella of Todos Santos was a Las Soldaderas. They performed numerous duties in the military, and often fought the way the men fought. For a good account of the Las Soldaderas see the book, Poniatowska, Las Soldaderas: women of the Mexican Revolution. La Coronella of Todos Santos was a "Las Soldaderas," or a woman of the Mexican Revolution. They gave support to the troops of the Revolution where ever it was needed.

'It is easy to see why soldaderas are so likeable. No matter how bad things get, each man will always have his little soldaderas at his summons, to take care of him, to love him and to give him a gift once in a while. "It could be a drink of water or tequila or a round of ammunition." The soldaderas were depicted in the Mexican film La Cucaracha. Poniatowska, Las Soldaderas : Women of the Mexican Revolution, Cinco Punta Press El Paso 2006. pp38,16. La Coronella went beyond the call of duty. She often fought beside the men of the Revolution. It was said she could "out shoot" most men and, out drink them.

For more first-hand information on "La Coronella," or the colonel, consult a book by Hagus "Treasure of Todos Santos" p 117. Hagus is a good source of everyday life in Todos Santos as it was lived by locals. The revolution of 1910, p.35. There is a description of the ambush and death of Pancho Villa. Hagus, p 38.

The Mexican revolution was coming to an end in the early 1920's. Pancho Villa surrendered and settled to live on a ranch in northern Mexico. The revolution battle war "Cry Mexico for the Mexicans." Land reform was taking place. Mexico was for the Mexicans. The inequalities, and the injustices, and the helpless poverty, of the past could the rich no longer be accepted. Independence from the past could no longer be accepted." Independence from the land lords had taken place. The revolution of 1910 was over. Brenner, The Wind that swept Mexico, U of Texas press, p 62-63 1971.

Zapata was assassinated in 1919 because he defied the Carranza government and would not disarm. Carranza ordered the federal forces to carry out the assassination.

Pancho Villa was assassinated in 1923, Villa had an ongoing dispute with the Herrera family which dated back many years to the revolution. Jesus Herrera planned the assassination. The federal government looked the other way. Pancho Villa was visiting a nearby village when he was shot fourteen times while driving his prized auto.

The most famous historians about the history of Todos Santos was the late professor Nestor Agundez Martinez. It was said that if you wanted to know anything about the history of Todos Santos "Go see professor Nestor." He always had time for questions. He also served as the director of the cultural center, Hagus, p55. The hotel California has an important played role into shaping the history of Todos Santos.

The hotel was founded in 1948 by a Chinese immigrant named Mr. Wong. Locals called him "El Chino, "or the Chinaman." The hotel California had a restaurant and bar. The first in Todos Santos Mr. Wong transported ice to the hotel from La Paz in the 1950's. Later Mr. Wong opened the first gas station. Some people think the Eagles song, "Hotel California" was written about the hotel in Todos Santos. No one is sure. But it makes a good legend.

Eventually the hotel was purchased and restored by a Canadian couple, John and Debbie Stewart. John, I am sorry to report passed away a few years ago. But they put the Hotel California back on the map. It is the center of all tourist activity in Todos Santos. I met Debbie on my last trip to Todos. She was working around the front desk. She gave me a few minutes to discuss the history of the hotel and the controversy of the song. She also had some ghost stories if you see her. Today Todos Santos prospers from farming, fishing and ranching. Tourism has been increasing in visitors because of the paved road from Cabo San Lucas. Artisans have relocated in Todos Santos and opened hand craft shops and galleries. A little modern bohemia.

Todos Santos was named a "Pueblo Magico" in 2012. This is a special recognition given to cities by the Mexican tourist's bureau to places which offer visitors a "magical" experience" because of their natural beauty, cultural riches, and historical importance. The traveler should put Todos Santos on your must see list. It is a jewel in the desert I always look forward to visiting. Historically, the cape of Baja developed faster than Todos Santos for the competition of tourists. Then in1956 the hotel Pamilla come to Cabo San Jose. Many Hollywood people traveled to Pamilla. It was a charming hotel in a beautiful natural setting. The owner of Pamilla "Bud Parr" built a resort in Cabo San Lucas. In 1959, Parr opened the hotel Cabo San Lucas. Parr also built an air strip.

When reading Baja Legends by Nieman I learned of some of the famous people who visited Baja in the early twentieth century. Norte Americanos started to travel to Baja when. "Fly Ins" Were popular in the 1950's. Air strips were built by the hotels.

John Wayne became a frequent visitor to Baja. Other visitors were Orson Wells, Bing Crosby, Desi Arnaz, Lucile Ball, Charlie Chapman, Babe Ruth, Wallace Berry, Jean Harlon, and John Barrymore. They were putting Baja on the map. The first hotel in Cabo San Lucas was the hotel Cabo San Lucas. A small hotel completed in 1959. Cabo only had a small population of 500 people.

The hotel had its s own power plant. An airstrip was built. John Wayne was one of many Hollywood movie stars who came to Baja. There are many stories about visiting celebrities who helped to put Baja on the map. See Niemann, Baja legends. My John Wayne story about Baja Cabo San Lucas history. First let me say that like many people John Wayne was my hero.

His war movies inspired all of us and raised money for war bonds. On one of my many trips to Cabo San Lucas. I dined frequently at the Crazy Lobster on Calle Hidalgo. I got to know the elderly woman owner who told me this story. In the old days John Wayne dined there frequently. After dinner and drinks he played cards with locals. He loved cards. He would play cards until the late hours. She kept the place open for him. Commenting on John Wayne, she said "he was a big man with broad shoulders, very impressive. He wore a large cowboy hat," she said. When he took his hat off she was amazed to see he was bald. I suppose in "the true grit he wore a toupee? But it happens to all of us. He is still to many of us a great man. John Wayne was a frequent visitor to Baja. Wayne enjoyed dove hunting of course, fishing was the main attraction.

Cary Grant also was a Visitor. He loved the solitude which he probably could not find today in Cabo. My favorite hotel is the Hotel Sea of Cortez. It was built in 1972, and still continues to attract visitors year around. It is in downtown and has been renovated. It is still a travel bargain. I stay there in all my trips to Cabo.

In Todos Santos stay at either the hotel California, on Casa Tota. Todos Santos was selected in 2009 as one of Mexico elite magic towns, or Pueblos Magicos. This honor is given by the Mexican Tourism secretary. Towns selected into the program have access to federal funds for public relations and improvements. Towns are selected because of their cultural and historical contributions to Mexico. The size of the town does not matter. Todos Santos is proud of this honor.

2

The appeal of Todos Santos why visit?

"We live in a wonderful world that is full of beauty, charm and adventure. There is no end to the adventure we can have if only we seek them with our eyes open."

–Jawaharial Nehra

Todos Santos has been a "hidden jewel" in the desert of Baja Mexico. But no longer. Tourist have discovered Todos Santos and are traveling there in greater numbers on the new highway 19 either from Los Cabos or La Paz. Although I am happy to report the crowds are not as massive as you see in Cabo San Lucas.

Todos Santos early on was more prosperous by the sugar cane mills. It was the sugar cane capital of Baja. It was much like colonial Mexico. Today Todos Santos is attracting surfers and artists and ex-patriots especially from the USA, are moving to Todos Santos to retire or open a business. The town has numerous festivals such as the music or film festival which attract tourist. It is popular for a day trip from Cabo, or La Paz. Sugar mills "molinos" are being replaced by art galleries, gourmet restaurants, and shops.

Some come to sleep one night at the famous Hotel California. It appeals to those who want to see what "Old Mexico" was like. Baja as a whole attracts the fisherman, and in the winter the whale watchers. Eco tourism in popular. Jacques Cousteau describes the Sea of Cortez as "a living aquarium."

The golfer has numerous choices to play on the courses in the corridor between San Jose and Cabo San Lucas BCS. Todos Santos today is slowly changing. It is no longer a sleepy village in the desert. Instead, it is a vibrant oasis in the desert with a bright future as a tourist attraction. Eco tourism is sprouting. Especially whale watching and the release of turtles back to the ocean is a growing attraction for eco-tourists. We have only one planet earth, and we must protect it from environmental deterioration. Mexico is doing their part in ecotourism.

Why I like BCS? The places, colonial architecture, nature, mountains and the ocean, and the people. The Mexican people are mild mannered, helpful, curious, and friendly. Take your time to visit the people. Try speaking Spanish. Learn the culture. Learn where to travel and things to do. It is a world of adventure, and learning. Travel is a University!

3

Hotels and where to sleep in Todos Santos BCS

"Do not follow where the pathway may lead.
Go instead where there is no path and leave
the trail."
                              -Ralph Waldo Emerson

Todos Santos, because of highway 19, has become a final
destination for those who want to experience history,
artisans, fishing, and surfing. Continue on highway 19
to reach La Paz on the Sea of Cortez. Many people come
to Todos Santos to retire. Hotels have begun to sprout
up, especially along the Juarez Calle in El Centro. This
is where you will find the famous Hotel California. Price
ranges for hotels go from budget class, moderate, and to
luxury depending upon your preference. In this book I
try to offer you a wide variety in Todos Santos, and Baja
BCS California.

Some are close to the beach, but none are far away.

On the internet, I prefer using booking.com, Priceline, or Trivago, your choice Amigos!

Hotel California, This small downtown hotel is frequently visited by tourists who are just on a day trip. It is not far from Ado autobus station. Prices range from 105-to 189 USD. The original hotel California was built in 1948 by El Chino, a member of a Chinese immigrant family. Much later it was purchased by a Canadian couple, John and Debbie Stewart, and was last renovated in 2003. The song by the Eagles made the hotel a popular destination. It is not known for sure if the Eagles even spent the night there. But it will be forever immortalized in history. The location is central. There is a swimming pool, La Coronella restaurant, souvenir shop, and a patio bar with live music. There is a Sunday brunch. The walls are colorful, and covered in paintings. It is just a beautiful place to walk through. Some people claim they have seen ghosts at night. Just let your imagination run wild. Contact hotel California directly at telephone 612-145-0525, or on the Internet at www.hotelcalifornia.com. A must see when in Todos Santos.

John Stewart called the pueblo "A little jewel in the middle of the desert." At the top of the line in Todos Santos is the Rancho Pescadero on the beach, or la playa located at Camino la playa, El Pescadero BCS 23300. There are 27 rooms, prices range from 180-400 USD. Rooms have ocean views. There are yoga classes too! They have their own organic garden and restaurant contact them at telephone 612-135-5849, or www.ranchopescadero.com. Many ocean activities are available.

There is surfing, boogie boards, sea kayaking, fishing, and yoga. A complete ocean resort.

One of my favorite hotels in Todos Santos is Casa Tota hotel. Located at Calle Alvaro Obregon, Todos Santos Baja California Sur 2330 Mexico. Telephone number 1-866-599-6674. It has fifteen rooms on two floors. There is a small swimming pool, bar and restaurant. Also, an outdoor patio with bar and food service. The average cost is 90-100USD. A great location and value it has AC and TV, Irma Burgos is the manager. The hotel is within walking distance to numerous shops, restaurants, and bars. The cathedral Pillar and the plaza are an easy walk.

Another favorite hotel of mine in Todos Santos is the Posada La Poza, on the lagoon and off the beach. The address is Camino a La Poza 282 Col La Poza, Todo Santos, Baja California Sur 2330 Mexico telephone number +52 612 145 0400 or www.lapoza.com email address is reservations@lapoza.com. Lapoza is owned by Juerg and Libusche Wiesendanger, two former bankers. From Zurich Switzerland. On a trip to Todos Santos they were impressed with the climate and location. They decided to leave the corporate world. They broke ground in June 2000 and open the hotel in 2002. La poza has a saltwater swimming pool and a small beach on the Pacific. The views of the lagoon and ocean are impressive. The sunsets from the deck bar are unforgettable. A room at the La poza will cost $140.00 USD. The owners have their own art galleries where they display this personal works of art. Posada La Poza has a gourmet restaurant named La Gusta.

In Cerritos you can stay at hotel Olas De Cerritos

if you are looking for a budget hotel near the beach and a short drive to Todos Santos. It is just off Highway 19 south of Todos Santos. Rooms are just $80.00 USD. It has only eight rooms. Wi-Fi is complementary. It is popular with surfers.

More expensive are the Villas De Cerritos located at 500 Cerritos beach highway 19 El Pescadero. Todos Santos 23000 Mexico. Priced at $349.00 USD. If you want luxury and location this is for you.

A new hotel in Cerritos is the Hacienda Cerritos. It is built high on the cliffs with a spectacular view of the Pacific Ocean at the North end of Cerritos beach. It is an expensive boutique hotel. Popular with whale watchers. The oceanfront bar is open to the public. Many people go here to see whales during whale watching months. December to March annually.

Additional hotel choices in Todos Santos: Casa Bentley $170.00 USD 1-866-298-0996 located in the historic district just off the plaza. Heated pool.

Hotel Guaycura, located in the center of Todos Santos is a boutique hotel with terrace. Rooms have private terrace beach club facilities with transportation Telephone number 1-877-448-2928 or +52(612)175 0800 email address is reservations@guaycura.com $109.00 USD. Todos Santos Inn $125.00USD a restored brick colonial building. Antique furniture, private terraces, air-conditioning La Copa bar +52(612)145 0040 www. todossantosinn.com.

Posada Del Molino telephone number +52(253) 719 5500 locals call 145-0471.$90.00 USD air-conditioning television and pool. www.posadadelmolino.com Molino is the word for the sugar mill.

Surfers Hostel Calle Bravo 36 Barrio San Ignacio, Todos Santos. $49.00 USD free Wi-Fi a shared kitchen, tour desk, and terrace, private bathroom. Located near La Esquina Cafe.

Pescedero surf camp cabanas at highway 19 km 64 Todos Santos +52(612) 130 3032 www.percederosurf. com surf board rentals and lessons.

The Hotelito, combine elegance and style with air-conditioning, wi-fi connection, saltwater pool. www. thehotelito.com Telephone number +52(612) 145-0099. $125.00 USD exceptional value, includes breakfast. If you are still confused about where to stay then Google the websites for information about Todos Santos hotels, vacation rentals, activities, shops and restaurants at info@ todossantos.com +52(612) 141 7026. This site is the information source for Todos Santos and Pescedero.

Vaya con dios amigos! Happy Travels!

4

The Eagles song "Welcome to the Hotel California." The legend myth or reality?

Hotel California "plenty of room at the hotel California."

–Don Felder, The Eagles.

The song "Hotel California" has become an urban legend. It is not sure it was written about the hotel California in Todos Santos. But there was no hotel California in L.A. The controversy goes on even today. The song was written in the 1970s by Don Henley. As the song became popular the legend grew. Don Henley in an interview said that he has never stayed at the hotel California. But, how do you explain the lyrics which reflect this area of Baja? Example, "cool wind in my hair, or "I heard the mission bell?" Also," the smell of colitas?"

In 2001, John and Debbie Stewart, Canadians, purchased the hotel. Full scale renovation was made. John

Stewart has passed away. I spoke with his wife Debbie, who is the manager now. She dismissed the controversy and did not understand the purpose of the controversy. On my final stay on Sunday afternoon a band played in the courtyard. Their last song was "Hotel California." You could close your eyes and visualize the history which took place there. I suggest that each person believe what they choose. Personally, I am a romantic and like to think it is "The Hotel California." In my mind it always will be. It is as John Stewart once said "A little jewel in the desert." Let it always remain. "So I called up the captain, please bring me my wine. He said, we haven't had this experience here since 1969." The Eagles. Azlyrics.com Glenn Fry, a founder of Eagles, and a guitarist died in 2016 as I write this book.

5

Restaurants, and dining
in Todos Santos

Restaurants, and dining in Todos Santos. "If,
you reject the food, ignore the customs, fear
the religion, and avoid the people, you might
better stay home."

-James A Michener

Tourists in Todos Santos have many choices for dining,
regardless of the mealtime. You can choose from small
cafés (cocinas) to elegant dining and hotels. There are
even cafés in the shops of artisans. Taco stands on the
roadside are popular. Seafood is an abundant and popular
since Todos is on the ocean. Fish is harvested from the
Pacific and shrimp from La paz and the Sea of Cortez.
Tacos are a way of life. Food lovers will enjoy Todos
Santos. The basic foods in Mexico are corn, beans and
chili peppers. Tortillas can also be added to the list. The
Spanish introduced the fusion of beef, pork, chicken and
goat. Dairy products such as cheese were also introduced.

The Maya already had tomatoes, squash, avocados and cocoa. Also, there were tropical fruits such as guava, pear, banana and mango. Organic farming is now popular, also local organic herbs. Seafood (pescado) such as marlin, el dorado, swordfish, snapper, tuna, shrimp and octopus are found throughout Baja. Fish is usually served with chili pepper salsa and a side of rice. Seafood soup is called "Sopa de mariscos," is popular. This soup can be made with any combination of seafood, such as fish and shrimp and sometimes with octopus.

One of the best restaurants for tacos is El Zaguan in Todos. Fish and shrimp are their specialties. They use fresh ingredients and sauces. The restaurant is in an old colonial building with rustic tables. There is also a bar. It is open for lunch and dinner. They advertise the "Best fish in town." Vegetarian dishes are also available. Telephone number +52 612 145 0485 Monday-Saturday 12-9pm. The location is on Calle Juarez between Hidalgo and Topete prices are moderate.

Organic farming has become popular in Todos and Baja south. You may be staying long term and cooking for yourself. Many restaurants now offer an organic section on their menu. Driving into Todos from Cabo you will see rows and rows of organic agriculture. An organic salad with goat cheese is popular. To purchase organic food, and produce, visit Lizzaraga Mercado. It is located near the hotel Casa Tota on the corner of Militar and Obregon. The farmers market (Mercado local) is popular on Wednesdays it is located at La Esquina, Todos Santos.

The organic market is located on Calle Marquez de leon across from Alma Tamales, Todos Santos. The best place to purchase fresh fish is from the fishermen at Punta Lobos, it is called fishermen's Beach. The fishermen ride their panga boats on the waves onto the beach about 1 to 3pm daily. Turn off highway 19 at 54km just south of Todos follow Calle Francisco west to the beach.

If you prefer, you can buy your groceries at a Mercado, such as super Mercado el sol located on degollado. Another Mercado is Mercado Guluarte on morelos just before Juarezin el centro Todos Santos.

Miguel restaurant highway, 19 el centro, Todos Santos BCS Mexico this is a traditional Mexican restaurant and a modest setting which makes it interesting. Prices are affordable. A favorite of the locals, some say the chile relleno is the very best. The seafood is the fresh catch of the day. Miguel and his family own and manage the restaurant. This may be your best value in Todos Santos.

The Sandbar in Pescadero, is a good place to go on Friday and Saturday nights. It is considered one of the best sports bars in the area the dress code is ultra-casual. Many locals hang out there. Some do not wear shoes since it is a sandbar. There is a happy hour weekdays 3 PM to sunset. On Wednesday night there is live music and all-you-can-eat pizza. The kids can fill up here cheap. They also serve lunch and dinners. Ask for Helen the owner or Gabe the bartender telephone number +52 612 130 3209 location highway 19, Km63, Pescadero, BCS Mexico. It is very close to the Pemex gas station.

Restaurant Tre Galline 33 Centenario and Topette Todos Santos BCS Mexico telephone number +52 612 145 0274 the owners are from northern Italy. Angelo is the chef and uses only fresh fish such as snapper and locally grown organic vegetables, of course there they are Italian items on the menu such as ravioli, lasagna and pasta dishes. Don't forget the shrimp. Prices are moderate. They offer Mexican wine which comes from Baja Valley of Guadalupe.

A nice alternative is the deli Todos Santos. It is located across the street from Bancomer bank near the hotel California at the corner of Juarez and Morelos. They offer subs and sandwiches and also salads and pastries are on the menu. Coffee, Latte and juice are popular. There is a full bar with wine, and over 72 different brands of beer. Telephone number +52 612 121 5889 email delisantitos@ live.com.

A less expensive restaurant is the bar and restaurant Bob Marlin. Located on Juarez El Centro, 23300 Todos Santos. Telephone number +52 612 214 79232. They advertise it is like being on the beach without leaving the center of Todos Santos. They have TVs for watching sports. There is a happy hour from 6 to 8 PM. They are known for their cold beers and margaritas. Tacos are their specialty they offer a 99 cent taco special you get three tacos and a margarita. Also, on the menu is the catch of the day. The bar stays open until 12 midnight. Most bars close at 9 or 10 PM so if you need a late night drink Bob Marlin is the place.

One of the most expensive restaurants in Todos Santos is the Café Santa Fe. They advertise it as "simply the best." Located at Calle Centenario 4 centro, 23300 Todos Santos BCS Mexico telephone number +52 612 145 0340. The Café Santa Fe is an authentic Italian food restaurant and a beautifully renovated 1850s colonial building. It has served quality food for 24 years. One of the owners is from northern Italy. They grow their own organic produce. Their pizzas are cooked in a wood fire oven. Seafood and meats are also served.

La Santena restaurant in the hotel Casa Tota. Calle Alvaro Obregon, 23300 Todos Santos Mexico. My hotel on this trip was the Casa Tota. I found that the quality of the food to be excellent and the prices moderate. Therefore I took most of my meals in the La Satena, on the outside patio. They offer breakfast, lunch and dinner. La Santena menu. My favorite was organic salad with goat cheese MXN 105 other menu items are chile relleno 116, catch of the day 151, seafood soup 110, and nacho 99. Margaritas 70, beer 31, and wine 82 MXN.

El Gusto restaurant in the hotel posada La Poza telephone number +52 612 145 0400 Lapoza.com or email is reservations@lapoza.com located at Camino a La Poza 282 col. LaPoza, Todos Santos BCS 23300 Mexico From El centro drive west, south of the palm trees. Follow Carrillo, take a left and turn right on Camino de la Poza. Follow until you see Posada la Poza next to the lagoon. The owners and on-site managers are Juerg and Libusche Wiesendanger who are originally from Switzerland. After a career in banking and numerous trips to Baja they settled upon living in Todos Santos.

They like the weather since it is spring like weather all year. Also, they like the people and laid back atmosphere. They saw a need for a hotel and restaurant near the beach. The wife is an artist and they would fit in well with the art colony. They opened in early 2002. The wife has an art gallery with her many paintings. The restaurant is named

El Gusto. It is known as a Mexican gourmet menu with an international fusion. The produce is organic and they have the freshest seafood. They offer vegetarian as well. You can choose to be seated on the whale deck or Sunset Terrace. They have an array of Mexican wine. The bar is a roof top and offers excellent views of the lagoon and the ocean,. or whale watching using your binoculars, and zoom lens.

The Garden restaurant at Rancho Pescadero, Todos Santos, Baja Mexico. Ranchopercadero.com telephone number +52 612 135 5849 address Parcela 53, El Pescadero, Todos Santos 23000 Mexico. Just turn right (west) at the Pemex and follow the road to the Pacific. continue Baja beans driving south from Todos. You will know when you have arrived. The garden comes into view. Rows and rows of vegetables, produce, and herbs. They grow and harvest their own. The chef Rodrigo Bueno. He prides himself is the freshest. Whether from the garden or from the ocean. He cooks from an open kitchen for all to see. The specialty of the garden is the Baja shrimp with spices. The specials change every day. The vegetables are fresh from the garden. The dinner will be one to remember. Don't forget the margarita!

La Coronella restaurant in the Hotel California. The chef is the well-known Dany Lemonte from Belgium. They offer organic vegetables and classic Mexican dishes such as chiles rellenos. There are omelets, angus burgers, and lamb burgers. Smoked marlin and pizza. Enjoy the courtyard fountain and live music. I am sure you will hear Hotel California.

Tequila sunrise bar and grill. Calle Juarez, Todos

Santos telephone number +52 612 145 0073. The Hotel California is across the street. The menu is local Mexican cuisine. A specialty is the shrimp Chile rellenos. The chef uses only fresh ingredients. Customers have about the margaritas. The flan desert is recommended. The value is moderate to pricey.

Baja beans roasting company. Carreta 19 km 63 El Pescadero, Todos Santos Telephone number +52 612 130 3297. The owner Alec and April, are from Vancouver, Canada. Baja beans is south of Todos near Cerretos hwy 19. Outdoor dining is available. www.bajabeans.com. Baja beans offers fresh roasted coffee, espresso, mochas, and latte. Also, pastries, such as fresh baked scones, biscuits, muffins, and cakes. There is a popular community market on each Sunday.

"Shut up" frank's sports bar and grill. Avenida Santos Degolldo near the Pemex gas station. Todos Santos Baja telephone number +52 612 145 0707. A popular gringo sports bar and grill. Not pricey. Rates are for the average local citizen and expatriot The hamburgers and fish and chips are the best. Cervezas are cold. They also have a Mexican menu, and lobster. Happy hours are Monday-Fridays. The TV dish network is elaborate. Norte Americans come here to see their favorite football team, and Europeans come to see their soccer, or football. Great place to watch sports!

La Esquina Eco café and bar. It is sometimes overlooked because of its location. But locals and expatriots know it well. The address is Calle Topete and Horozonte, or locally called "the corner." It is also an internet café in the daytime. Oscar and Paula discovered the unique location while walking to the beach. They wanted an eco-café with their own garden. They found the perfect location at "the corner." The La Esquina has its own garden for fresh produce. There is a farmers market on the grounds on Wednesdays. Breakfast is a popular meal here for locals, expats, and tourists. It is similar to a coffee shop for breakfast. The coffee is strong Mexican. They have a fresh fruit, salad, pastries and blueberry pancakes. The food is good and the menu is not pricey. It has a great local feel. The atmosphere is relaxed. Lunch and dinner is popular with customers and quesadilla are 65mx, enchiladas 85mx, burrito wrap 20mx, organic salads 60mx, and hamburger and fries 100mx. There are healthy sandwiches and salads. At night La Esquina offers live music. The music can be Mexican, or reggae. One night a week they have the "night of madness." Local talent is highlighted if you want to feel like a local then La Esquina is the place for you.

The distillery a retail seller of alcohol on Calle Hidalgo, Todos Santos Baja telephone number +52 612 145 0098 email spirits@thedistillery.mx. Also, take out is available. First artisan distillery in Baja Sur. The distillery produces homemade whiskey, vodka, and tequila. Tastings are offered daily. There is a full service restaurant. Wine La Bodega de Todos Santos. Calle Hidalgo at Juarez and Militar telephone number +52 612 152 0181.

La Bodega has a wide selection of wines for a town the size of Todos. There are nightly wine tastings with local food and musician. On Mondays there are complementary tapas. Mac the manager is very knowledgeable about the wines. Most Mexican wines come from North Baja in the

Valley of Gandeloupe, or San Viante. Wine aficionados should not miss a visit to LaBodega.

Landi's restaurant Legaspi NO.15, next door to the theater Marqnez de leon just off the Plaza at city center. This is the most authentic Mexican food in Todos. Family operated restaurant. Chile relleno is the best on the inexpensive menu.

Taco George Todos Santos, locals call this the best "taco" in Todos Santos. Also, it is a good value at 15mx pesos. This family owned roadside taco stand specializes in the fish taco. Fish are caught daily at Punta Lobos. They have a loyal following. Taco George can be found on Calle Militar underneath a blue canopy. They have plastic tables and chairs. You cannot beat the quality and price. Your best bet if you are on a rock bottom budget.

Dana's Diner features old-fashioned food with old-fashioned prices. Probably the best buy in Todos. They serve up hamburgers, fries, and onion rings. Located in Peradero next to Pemex and Oxxo, km62.5 Telephone number +52 612 130 3363.

The number of local restaurants in Todos Santos continue to grow each year. Along with the growth comes the reputation of the chefs who either live here or move here. Traditional Mexican food is still the king in Todos. But the popularity of the fusion of traditional Mexican with organic grown fresh produce and vegetables makes it mark. Of course, seafood is readily available. Don't forget the peppers and spices. It has all come together to create what is uniquely Todos Santos Baja cuisine.

6

Whale watching in Todos Santos and Baja

"Take only memories, leave only footprints."
-Chief Seattle.

Whale watching is one of the most popular activities in Baja. Each year various species of whale travel 7000 miles from Alaska south along the Baja coast to mate, or to have their baby calves in the warm waters of the lagoons.

They travel in groups called pods. The whales are mostly Gray California whales. Also, "humpback" whales. Some whales, such as the humpback go further south and turn the tip of Cabo, and go into the sea of Cortez to either Loreto, or LaPaz. These include the elusive Blue whales. On my trip I saw mostly humpbacks whales off the coast of Cabo near the arch. What an exciting experience to see the whales up close and to interact! You will see them breach, spy hopping, feeding their calves, or just playing. A lifetime experience I highly recommend it to anyone.

The gray whales once were near extinction because of hunting. Today there are over 20,000 because of protective laws by Mexico and the USA. It is said that the interaction with the whales is more up close and intimate in the lagoons above and below Todos Santos, such as Guerro Negro, or Magdalena lagoon.

Gray whales seem as if they are proud to show off their new calves. Remember, whales are mammals. Sometimes the tourists can touch or kiss a whale. Ojo de Liebre lagoon, or Scammon's lagoon is a well know breeding lagoon for the California gray whale on the west coast of Baja. Scammon was a whaler who slaughtered many whales for the whale oil. Today the lagoon is a prime viewing lagoon to see the mother whale and the newborn calf. Today the gray whale is a friendly whale. The hunting days are over. The whales are safe.

The mothers even push their calves up close to the boat to see the curious tourists. In Todos Santos the best way to go whale watching is with La Sierra co-adventurer. November to March is the best time to see whales. I was there in February and there was an abundance of whales.

La Sierra Eco address is La Sierra Eco adventures, Calle Olachea S/N, Todos Santos, BCS CP 2330, Mexico. Telephone +52 612-145-0353 US telephone 213-265-9943 or just google them and they will arrange a whale watching tour.

The panga (small boats) launch from Puntas Lobos. It is best to go in the mornings. Rates are per charter 275.00 per charter of five people. Sometimes they can pair you up with a group. You can use Pay Pal to pay. The great whales gather in three lagoons primarily. On the West Coast of Baja there are Scammon's lagoon, San Ignacio lagoon, and Magdalena Bay. The lagoons are a protected area by the Mexican government and provide a safe haven for the whales to reproduce. The travel companies can book a whale watching encounter for you. They use a small boat in the lagoons to transport the tourists. The government limits the number of boats to enter the watching area. Each has no more than 6 to 8 tourists, a guide and a boat handler. This can be booked in Todos Santos including tours to LaPaz and the Sea of Cortez. During the peak season Scammon's lagoon can have a population of 1000 whales. Because of the large numbers of whales it is most likely the tourists will be able to touch a whale. Even the newborn calves are friendly. The whales are curious and friendly mammals. It is truly amazing and what a great experience! Some travel companies can organize sea kayaking trips to see the whales. They offer tented camps, or stays in small hotels as part of the package.

Baja Jones adventure travel offers gray whale vacations using upscale tented camps during the migration season. They call it "the most comfortable tent accommodations on any Baja Ocean Baja shore." Baja Jones was given a five-star rating by trip advisor.

Keith Jones, from the USA, is the founder of Baja Jones adventures. Jones says that "since 1992 Baja Jones has logged over 3000 hours of observing the whales of Baja while sitting in the panga." He is very knowledgeable of the subject of Baja whales. Jones even has a book on the subject, Gray whales, my 20 years of discovery, Keith E Jones, the book is available on Amazon. Keith Jones, Baja adventures, is located 14812 West Maui Ln. Surprise AZ 85379 USA Telephone number 562-889-4016. Keith@graywhale.com office in USA 626-252-9759. Be sure to sign up for the free newsletter. His five-day trip is the most popular.

Miramas adventures in San Diego USA is another option to book a whale watching tour in Baja. They offer trips to the Pacific side, La Paz and the sea of Cortez. They have kayaking trips, and motorboats. Lodging is in local hotels. It is small group travel. Todos Santos Eco adventurer offers a two-day whale watching tour in Magdalena Bay. The observer gets to pet and interact with gray whales in Baja. Small panga boats are used. This gives you maximum interaction with the whales. The price is 375USD per person. Includes guide and RT transportation from hotel. Magdalena Bay is also a breeding ground for birds and sea lions. A hotel in San Carlos is included. The contact address is Cerro La Poza, 23300, Todos Santos, BCS, Mexico telephone number +526121450189.

Pachcos Ecotours La Paz Baja is another tour organizer you will see gray whales. Gray whales are found in the sea of Cortez on the east side of Baja. You can take the Aguila bus or fly there. Pachcos can make complete arrangements. Pachcos travels to San Ignacio lagoon for whale watching. They have cabins, and serve meals. Often with the gray whale you can touch or kiss them.

For my whale watching adventure I selected Cabo Expeditions, only a short drive south of Todos Santos. They use pangas like they used in films by Jacques Cousteau. They book small groups of six or eight. Small groups allows for a better experience, especially if you are taking photos, or videos. The price is 69USD as a single. I got some great photos. My friends marvel over the action shots. I was totally satisfied. It is Cabo's best whale watching tour in my opinion. I like the pangas and the guides are experts. They seem to know the best spots to watch whales, especially humpbacks. Contact Cabo Expeditions at www.caboexpeditions.com.mx. US & Canada toll free 619-752-2294 Mexico telephone +52 162 4143 2700 Blvd. Marina, INTL. hotel Wyndham, Cabo San Lucas, BCS.

I have been to Baja for numerous trips, whale watching is truly an unforgettable adventure. You will remember your experience to see the whale migrating with their newborns. Frolicking in the water. Sometimes approaching the pangas. This experience ranks right up there with my trips to see elephants in Africa. What "a wonderful world" we have.

Save the whale Amigos Y Amigas!

Sea Turtles, Birding and Yoga

"Travel makes on modest. You see what tiny
place you occupy in the world."
                                    –Gustave Flaubert

Sea turtle volunteering can stay in the casita, or cabins
between Todos Santos and the beach for a fee. There is
a common kitchen in a palapa. Anyone can volunteer.
February to April are the best months for watching
releases. The volunteers and supervisors are here because
they have a common passion for the ocean, and inhabitants
of the ocean. The environmental experience is a positive
educational experience. It is environmental conservation
with sea turtle focus. The goal is to restore and maintain
the sea turtle population. Las Playitas beach is about 1.5
miles North of Todos Santos on the Pacific.

Tortugueros Las Playitas is a beach located between
Calle 105 Mangos Camino International Todos Santos
BCS M 2300 US telephone number 213-265-9943
Todos Santos telephone number 612-145-0353 email

tortugueroplayitas@gmail.com. Indicate in your message if you wish to volunteer or if on an internship.

Turtle eggs on my recent visit to Baja I came across the story in the Gringo Gazette, August 24, 2015 "Mama turtles" are beginning to arrive on the Pacific coast of Mexico, and so are the turtle egg thieves. They believe the turtle eggs will cure their sexual problems. Turtle eggs have been called the "poor man's Viagra." Police and army patrols have been sent out to safeguard the eggs. Two million eggs will be deposited upon the beaches by "mama turtles."

Bird watching Baja South is a major wintering area for birds from North America such as the hummingbird. There are also shorebirds to observe. A person can go birding on your own, or join a tour group. An option is to book with wings birding tours, The home office is located at 1643 N. Alverson suite 109 Tucson, AZ 85712 USA telephone number 1-866-547-9868 toll free. Matt Brooks, matt@wingsbirds.com. Ask for the tour Mexico: Baja California's Cape region. This is a complete natural history tour, with focus on the birds but also attention to the plants, reptiles, mammals, and insects found in Baja. The two include, trips to Todos Santos, Sierra Laguna Mountains, La paz, and Punta Colorada. The tour includes a visit to Magdalena Bay and Puerto San Carlos. Gray whales are seen on a four hour boat tour. Plenty of birds are seen along the way. The trip ends at Los Cabo airport for departure.

Eco adventures offers birding tours out of Todos Santos telephone number 612-145-0780 LaPoza Guaycura. Because of the proximity of the Pacific Ocean, mountains and mild climate Todos Santos has an abundance of activities. Just plan your time wisely either to explore on your own, or a group expedition. Surfing is king in Todos. Have fun amigos!

Find your Zen yoga is a holistic way of life. There are a variety of yoga classes available in Todos Santos. Many are available at Laarca, the community center on Topete Calle.

The Pachamama yoga retreat is a small retreat facing the Pacific. Where yoga is offered. Hotel rooms are provided in the total cost. Meals are mostly vegetarian or fish.

Pachamama yoga retreat is located at Camino Viejo and Camino Playitas. Telephone number 612-145-0477 or www.pachamamamexico.com. Pachamama also offers mountain biking, fishing, and surfing.

Yoga, as most people know, is about harmonizing the body with the mind and breathing techniques. Yoga was founded in India some 5000 years ago. The beautiful setting in the climate of Todos Santos facilitates discovering the harmony and self-awareness found in yoga.

Rancho Pescadero has a free yoga class every morning at 10 AM. Todos Santos is a great place to visit to relax.

However, there is an abundance of activities to choose from as you can see. It is the home of surfers, artists, yogis, fishing, whale watching and organic farmers. Sea turtle volunteering is an option for the individual. Volunteer if you have the time. Sometimes you can receive college credit. Save the sea turtle!

8

Sightseeing in Todos Santos

"Not all those who wanders are lost."
                                    -JRR Tolkien

Sightseeing in Todos Santos the historical and cultural history of old Todos Santos was largely shaped by the Spanish conquest of Mexico. The architecture is a good example, the food was also influenced. The geological setting near the Pacific was an important influence. The climate affected that agriculture. Plus the underground water supply.

Mission Nuertra senora del Pilar de Todos Santos was built in 1733. This was an Adobe building. Father Jaime Bravo established the mission, and was called Santa Rosa de Todos Santos.

Therefore the name "All Saints." The virgin of Pillar statue was located in the mission. The original Catholic church was built in 1747. This is the basics of the church you see today.

It has expanded over the years. The Cathedral is located in the Central Plaza at the corner of de leon and

Centenario. Todos Santos BCS 23305 MX telephone number 52 624-143-4180. Just up from the hotel California. A focal point for all tourists.

Centro cultural Nestor Agundez Martinez, or the house of culture Todos Santos. Located on Juarez two blocks up from the hotel California. The museum is located in a large brick home colonial style building which was once an elementary school. Nestor Agundez was the founder and director. He was a popular teacher. It is now a Museum of history and anthropology. The museum displays artifacts, and some murals. There are historic photographs and a public library. I am sad to say professor Nestor passed away in March 2009. He had played an important role in the shaping of Todos Santos, and in the education of local residents. Nestor has become an icon for Todos Santos.

The citizens will remember him forever. It was often said "if you want to know about the history of Todos Santos then go see professor Nestor."

Hotel California played a prominent role in the growth of Todos Santos. The history of the hotel dates back to 1947 when the first owner of the hotel, Antonio Wong Tabasco, or "El chino" purchased the colonial home to convert it into a hotel which he named hotel California. The hotel opened in 1950. "El chino" was the grandson of a Chinese immigrant. El chino also opened the first gas station. He was the first to transport ice from La Paz to Todos Santos. The song by the Eagles, "Welcome to the Hotel California" brought attention to the hotel and Todos Santos. There is controversy surrounding the song. Was it actually written about the hotel in Todos Santos?

The author of the song, Don Henley says it was not. But rather about the imaginary place in Los Angeles. The debate continues today. Still tourists come to visit the hotel. The last owner was a Canadian, John Stewart. Stewart purchased the hotel in 2001 and renovated the hotel. Stewart has passed, and his wife Debbie is now the owner and manager. In Todos Santos you will see many Molinos. Molinos were connected to the great sugar cane era from 1850 to 1950. Sugar cane played an important role economically in the development of Todos.

Molinos are tall chimneys and were part of the sugar cane processing mill. They are now considered historical structures in tribute to the period. There is a prominent Molino located at the Hotel Posada del Molino. Located just west of hwy. 19 and Rangel. Teatro Marquez de leon located near the mission Pilar at the end of de Leon.

The Aztec calendar is near by the theater. This was the first Theater in this part of the world. Today it is used for music concerts and dance performances. Casa Dracula. The house in Todos was constructed in 1852 by Antonio Dominguez, who had made his money in the sugar cane industry. It was first valued at 100,000 USD. The house is now owned by Norte Americanos who ask a price of 3.5 million USD for the property. It is a large two story home built in Spanish colonial tradition. It is called the Casa Dracula because of local rumors. When the house was not occupied it was said bats were seen flying in and out of the large house, some said it was a haunted house. It was also said gold and money were hidden in the house. But none was found. The Norte Americanos renovated the adobe brick home. They built a new floor upstairs and added some beams, and an additional bathroom. The house has four bedrooms and is used as a vacation retreat. Casa Dracula is located at Calle Topete and Horozonte, across from La Esqaina Café. Historical tours of Todos Santos are available.

You visit the historical buildings and get a feel for the history of the town and the region. It will give you a glimpse into the past, and what life was like. Ranchero tours is available, or a full day tour by taxi. Be sure to see Cerritos playa. The El Tecolote booksore is a popular place to buy history books, travel books, or maps. It is managed by an ex-patriot from the USA.

9

Art Galleries & Books

"The world is a book, and those who do not travel read only one page."

–Saint Augustine

Art galleries and books in Todos Santos is best known as a "Artist Colony." Charles Stewart, who is an ex-patriot, from New Mexico started the artistic movement. Now, there are numerous galleries all over Todos where they produce a variety of art. Many of the galleries are located on and around Calle Topete. Some are located in hotels while others occupy space and a restaurant, or a coffee shop. You will find a variety such as paintings, photographs, and ceramics, textiles, wooden and metal religious crosses, silver, and sculptures. Most are locally produced, and others come from different parts of Mexico and Guatemala.

The Charles Stewart gallery and studio is located at the corner of Calle Centenario and Obregon. Stewart paints mostly in watercolors, and oils. Sometimes he produces sculptures made from wood. He opened his studio in 1980 after moving from the USA. Telephone number 612- 145-0265 or email marischasart@yahoo.com.

Mangos folk art Todos Santos located Calle Centerario, near Topete and Obregon. Todos Santos in the historical district. Telephone number +52 612 145 0315. Mangosgaleria.com. Products by various local artists displays paintings, wood carvings, bags and textiles. The art comes from different places in Mexico. For those who love a broad selection for shopping, try Galleria de Todos Santos located Calle Legas and NO.33 North of Juarez. Feature regional artist of drawings, paintings and sculptures.

Founded in 1994 by Michael and Pat Cope, Telephone number +52 612-145-0500 or email galleriadetodossantos. com, has diverse styles great for the serious art collector. Galleria Indigo "Fine art Galleria." Calle Juarez near Calle Hidalgo and Topete. Near the bookstore telephone number 52 612 137 3473 or email indigotodossantos@ yahoo.com. Diaz Castro and Ezrakatz are the major artists on display. Galeria de Gabo features the work of artist Gabo from La Paz. Marquez de Leon, located between Juarez and Colegio militor Telephone number +52 612 145 0370 or email gaboartist@hotmail.com. They have paintings famous for their brilliant colors. The climate in Todos Santos is conducive to producing paintings in brilliant colors. Galleria Logan, Jill Logan is the owner, located Calle Juarez and Morelos. The paintings are mostly by Jill Logan an ex-patriot. She paints with oils and acrylics. Landscapes are her favorite. This galleria is considered one of the best in Todos Telephone number +52 612 145 0151. Jill Logan was educated in the USA at the University of Utah in fine arts. Her famous solo exhibition at the Galleria Logan was named "sensual women of the desert."1999.

Galleria wall, Catherine wall is the founder and owner since 1999. Wall paints scenes of Mexico specializing in landscapes and portraits in oil. Located at Calle Hidalgo at Rangel Centro Telephone number +52 145 0527.

Galleria La Poza located in the Hotel Posada La Poza Telephone number +52 612 145 0400 or visit galeriapoza. com Libusche Wiesdanger the wife and co-owner of the hotel manager, is in charge of the art gallery. Her paintings are exhibited on the walls of the hotel LaPosda.

Brillante Jewelry shop, Calle Centerario # 24 Calle between Calle Topete and Calle Obregon telephone number 52 612 145 0799 or email jbrillante@yahoo.com or visit www.brillante.com. I describe them as artists because they design most of their jewelry. They work in silver and gold.

El Tecolote Libros, or bookstore. Located corner of Hidalgo and Juarez. Just East of the Hotel California. Kate and Janet are the owners. They are ex-patriots from the USA. Telephone number +52 612 145 0295 or email katelewis@yahoo.com. It is unusual that a small town like Todos Santos has such an excellent bookstore. The selection is diverse. They also have maps of Baja which is one of their bestsellers. There is a coffee and juice bar in the store. I was shopping for a comprehensive book on the history of Todos Santos. I spoke with the manager since it seems there is no single book. She suggested, and I purchased a book by Hagus, Treasures of Todos Santos. This book is a collection of history stories by local residents who have seen the development of the Pueblo. The other book she suggested was Thetion, Legendary Hotel California. This book integrates the history of Todos Santos with the history of the hotel California. It is a valuable source of information about the growth of Todos Santos.

10

Shopping in Todos Santos

"Travel is the only thing you buy that makes
you richer."

-Anonymous

The number of shops in Todos Santos have grown
in recent years. Most of the shops are near the Hotel
California and are grouped around the main street of
Benito Juarez. There are usually displays of artisans in the
plaza across from the Pilar cathedral and the side streets
extending along Centenario and Leganpi. Some hotels
and restaurants have displays of art and works of artisans
for sale. The shops, or galleries offer various items ranging
from silver jewelry, cotton clothing for men and women,
blankets, paintings, ceramics, pottery, books and even
surfboards and related items for surfing. Many people
shop for silver crafts.

Most silver actually comes from Texco, a town of
artisans located near the silver mines near Mexico City. My
favorite silver store in Todos Santos is Brillante jewelry. It
is located Centeraro 24 Centro, 23300. It is between Calle

Topete and Calle Obregon telephone number 52 612 145 0494 or email jbrillante@yahoo.com. Ana Brillante was the founder she was known for her designs in silver. She created the famous "fan necklace" made especially for Eleanor Roosevelt.

Today her son, Jose, continues the famous designs. When you buy jewelry at Brillante's you are buying a collectible. It is on the expensive side but the quality is superior. Jose continues the famous collection of fan designs in silver. They make fan earrings 112.00USD, and fan bracelet is 317.00USD. The Family owned store is.

The Arte de Taxco. It is owned by the Vasquez family. They offer a large selection of silver work from Taxco. The store is located in plaza Las Farolen on Calle Juarez between Calle Marquez de Leon and Calle Hidalgo. Todos Santos, Baja, MX 23305. In the center of Todos Santos. In addition, they offer cotton clothing for both men and women, and children. Ceramics are also sold.

The largest jewelry store in Todos Santos is Pancho Jewelry. This shop is located near the hotel California on Calle Juarez between Morelos and Marquez. They offer silver from Taxco such as chains, and bracelets. You name it. They also sell popular copper art pieces. Casa Catalina corner of Calle Hidalgo next to Tecolote bookstore. Handmade pottery by locals.

The El Puebito Mexican sells fine opals. Next to the bus station on Calle Morelos. Ethnic Mexican art. Marquez de Leon. Todos Santos is a virtual shopper's paradise in a compact area. Many artisans are flocking to this small oasis in Baja Mexico. There is a variety of artisan shops, and art galleries. Most are located in the

El Centro cultural center of town. The small size of the "pueblo" makes it easy to walk from one shop to another. It is predicted that the number of galleries will only increase as time goes by. Happy shopping amigos! Remember to bargain.

> "You can have the money in your pocket, or the memories."
>
> –Clark Howard

Todos Santos Festivals

"Our happiest moments as tourists always seem to come when we stumble upon one thing while in pursuit of something else."

-Lawrence Block

Todos Santos is known for its festivals. The three most well-known are the music festival, the food and wine festival, and the CINE or movie festivals. Here is a list of the numerous festivals with approximate dates. Festival de musica, or music fest. January 16th, Festival de Arte, or art festival. January 16th, Festival de Cine, or Cinema Fest February 20th, Gastro vino Festival, or food and wine May 15th, Fiestas tradicionales, or festival of Senora del Pilar, the patron saint of Todos Santos. October 12th, annual house tour, March 15th, Mexican revolution day, popular throughout Mexico September 16th.

The Todos Santos music Festival was created in 2012 by rock musician Peter Buck, formally of R.E.M. the hotel California was one of the loyal sponsors. Buck loves Todos Santos. The annual music festival raises much-needed money for the Palapa Society for needy kids, and other charities.

The fiestas are popular with Norte Americanos, and Europeans. Each year the music fiesta has grown in popularity. Those who attend experience fantastic music and fun. Music shows can be found at the hotel California and the town Plaza. So make your reservations early and join the festival.

Here are the names of music groups who have attended: Chuck prophet, drive-by truckers, driving and crying, M. Ward and Dawer, and Peter Buck and his musicians. It varies each year. Local musicians are also given an opportunity to present their talent. Something for everybody. Last year the music festival raised 80,000 USD for charity. Peter Buck owns a home in Todos Santos.

Gastro vine festival (wine and food) April 24th, this festival celebrates annually the foods and wine of Baja California. The festival gives you an opportunity to taste food and wines from Baja. Also, you can meet local chefs from the array of popular restaurants. Appetizers are supplied by local restaurants. La Bodega is a major sponsor and supporter of the festival. Tickets can be purchased at La Bodega, or Tecolote bookstore. There will be a dinner in the Hotel California. Hotel California musicians will appear every day. At the festivals there will be bottles of wine for sale at special prices. Adam of La Bodega, Calle Hidalgo, is between Juarez and Colegio Militar, Todos Santos, Baja Sur 23300 Mexico Telephone number +52 612 162 0181 or visit www.gastrovino.mx. Wine tasting

M-Wed. 5-8pm Oct-Jun. It is reported that the manager, Mac, does generous pours.

Many people do not realize Baja produces some excellent wines, especially red wines in the Guadalupa valley. Baja also produces excellent olive oils. Be sure to subscribe to the newsletter www.fest300.com/magazine. This magazine will keep you up to date on the latest news.

El Festival de cine Todos Santos. Todos Santos film festival happens every March of each year. It is probably the most popular festival after the Revolution day festival. It is now in its eleventh year. The major venue is the Teatro Marquez de Leo. It is located at the corner of de Leon and Legaspi, almost next to mission del Pilar 23300 Todos Santos BCS telephone number 52 612 145 1083 or visit www.todossantoscinefest.com.

The film festival attracts directors and filmmakers from across Mexico, Latin America, Spain, and North America. They come here to screen their films. Most films have English subtitles and feature film discussions after the screenings. It is a week-long festival and is especially attractive to Latin American film winners. The film winners received the Golden cactus award as judged by the critics. Some 70 films are shown during the week-long event. There are documentaries, features, and shorts.

Art festival The Todos Santos art Festival occurs annually in early February. This is a week-long celebration of Mexican culture. Artisans from all over Mexico, and South America come to Todos to exhibit their art during this event. On display are paintings, photography, drawings, regional crafts, Mexican music, jewelry, leather, rugs and blankets. Folk dancing can be seen in the central Plaza. Displays of Mexican guitars for sale are included in tent displays. Mexican food such as tamales are for sale. Lectures on various subjects are available for attendance.

The art Festival is an excellent time to experience the culture and life of Mexico. Most exhibits and events are located in and around the central Plaza. Bring your dancing shoes. There are classes in case you cannot dance. This is one of the oldest and most popular festivals in Todos Santos. The Revolution day festival in Todos is most popular. It occurs on November 20th in the central Plaza. It is not to be confused with Cinco de Mayo which gringos or Norte Americans usually do not understand the difference. Cinco de Mayo was a battle fought in 1862 in Puebla Mexico near Vera Cruz. This was the Franco-Mexican war. The "ragtag" Mexican militia were able to turn back the larger French force. It was a great victory, but only one battle in a larger war. Today in Mexico it is a minor holiday. It is a bigger celebration in the USA and an excuse to drink Corona.

The Mexican revolution is more widely celebrated in Mexico than Cinco de mayo. It began in 1910 and ended in 1920. It was an internal conflict by the common people and small farmers to overthrow the landed rich and the systems of the Landifundias. To "reform" civil liberties and the right to own land. Pancho Villa and Zapata fought to overthrow President Diaz and give rights to the common people. Some historians call it a civil war. Either way it ended with a new constitution in 1917 which gave land ownership to small farmers and took land ownership from non-Mexicans. Some fighting continued until 1920.

La Coronella, of hotel California, fought for Poncho Villa and Zapata. People shout "Viva Mexico."! An important day to celebrate! More than Cinco de Mayo!

Festival Señora de Pilar Oct. 10th This festival celebrates the founding of Todos Santos in 1723 by the Jesuit priest. Streets around the main Plaza are filled with tables of food, games and musicians. Festival of Señora de Pilar. This festival occurs in early October each year. It is named for mission Nuestra Señora de Pilar church. She is the patron saint of Todos Santos. The festival include music, dancing, singing. Carnival rides, and performances in the central Plaza near the Cathedral. Some say Todos Santos is the home of "the world's best festivals." Pick the one you like and "let's have a fiesta!"

12

Cabo San Lucas BCS
Mexico Gringo paradise

"I haven't been everywhere but it's on my list."

–Susan Sontag

Cabo San Lucas began as a Spanish colonial village founded by Hernan Cortes after he received a report that a shipwrecked sailor told of a land south of California that was rich in gold and pearls. Cortes sent ships in 1535 to explore the new land. They found no gold, but they did find pearls. The town of La Paz was established on the sea of Cortez, or Gulf of California, east of the peninsula. Baja was now officially on the map.

In 1539, the Spanish explorer Francisco de Ulloa sailed south around the Cape, Cabo San Lucas was founded. Cabo San Lucas became a popular stopping point for Spanish ships as they sailed eastward from the Philippines. In Cabo San Lucas, they could resupply with water and supplies to continue their journey. They could also trade silk and spices from their trade routes in the Far East.

In the 1950s, Cabo became a place to see and be seen by Hollywood stars such as John Wayne, Bing Crosby, and Desi Arnaz. They rented a small plane and flew South along the Pacific coastline. The roads in Cabo were not developed. When the pilot saw no more land, it was time to land. Even today, Hollywood stars flock to Cabo. They go to Cabo Wabo night club and the beach. Today, Cabo has numerous golf courses, and sport fishing there will always be an attraction.

The Cape is called Finis Terra, or the end of the land. The distinctive arch, or El Arco is a popular tourist attraction. It can be reached by boat. Today, giant cruise ships stop in Cabo San Lucas. The Mar de Cortez is a good hotel choice for budget travelers. A standard single room with a patio overlooking the pool is fifty-one US dollars. The location is in El Centro Cabo San Lucas on Lazaro Cardenas and Vicente Guerrero. Telephone number +624 143 0232. It is an easy walk to the marina and numerous restaurants and bars. This hotel was built in 1958. It is a piece of history.

The Mar de Cortez has its own restaurant and bar, Baja peppers. It is popular with locals and gringos because of its large all-American breakfast for thirty-five pesos, or three dollars. The best deal in Cabo, this breakfast comes with three eggs, bacon, country fried potatoes, fruit, and toast. The Baja peppers is open for lunch and dinner. Also there is a daily happy hour with drink specials. Wine lovers will enjoy the wine cellar. They feature weekly dinner specials such as ribs, pasta, soup, and salad. Monday is ladies night, featuring 50% off the menu.

A Luxury hotel in Cabo San Lucas, is the ultra-luxury

resort at Pedregal. It is a five star hotel, or resort in Los Cabos. Its only rival in Los Cabos is the one and only Palmilla resort. Since this is a luxury hotel the room terraces range from 600 US to 1500 US suites are available. There is an on-site spa. The hotel overlooks the Pacific Ocean. Highly acclaimed restaurant, the El Farallon is located on site. It is said to be a romantic dining experience overlooking the Pacifico. Known for its fresh seafood. The contact address is the resort at Pedergal, Camino del mar, Cabo San Lucas BCS, 23455 MX. Telephone 624 103 4300, or toll free 844-733-7342. Expensive.

Finisterra Hotel Cabo San Lucas is a new hotel located on the hilltop overlooking the marina. The guests can walk to El Arco and lands' end. Blvd paseo de La Marina SN, Centro 23450, Cabo San Lucas BCS MX. Telephone number 624 145 6700. This is a five-star all-inclusive hotel. Rates range from 449 two 633 USD beautiful view expensive. The Bangalows hotel. This is a budget class hotel. It is a quaint little inn overlooking the marina. Blvd. Miguel Herrera, Cabo San Lucas BCS 23450 MX. Telephone number 624 143 5035 or visit www.thebungalows.com.

Across the street from the hotel Mar de Cortez is the famous Cabo Wabo bar and nightclub. This is the place for those who want to party like a Rockstar all night long.

Cabo Wabo is owned by Sammy Hagar, a rock star from the United States. It features live music and is located on Calle Lazaro Cardenas and Guerrero. Telephone number 624 143 1198. It is open nightly from 7 PM to 2

AM and include a restaurant. There is a happy hour from 9 AM to 4 PM.

One of my favorite places to go in Cabo is the Giggling Marlin bar and grill. They call it home of the skip and go naked. It is located on Boulevard Marina and Matamoros, not far from the marina telephone number 624 143 0606. Website gigglingmarlin.com. It features a nightly floor show, good margaritas, typical bar food, sports on the television, and Mexican food. The staff is friendly. There is a nightly floor show free of charge.

A must stop for anyone going to Cabo, day or night, is El Squid Roe Cabo, which has a great dance floor. It is party city and features rock and pop music. It is open daily from 8 PM to 4 AM. Dinner is served until 11:30 PM it is located on Boulevard Marina, and Plaza Bonita, Cabo San Lucas.

Baja Cantina in the marina is one of my favorite places for happy hour and watching the ships in the marina. It is a dockside bar with sports on TV that appeal to gringos. Baja Cantina features an all-day happy hour. The restaurant offers seafood and discounted bar snacks. Another favorite of mine for dining is the Crazy Lobster Bar and Grill. Open day and night, it is located on Hidalgo street across from Poncho villas. Telephone number +624 143 6535. Steaks, chicken, tacos, hamburgers, and BBQ ribs are offered at reasonable prices for family dining. It always seems to be crowded. If you catch fish and bring it to them, they will prepare it. For beach fun, go to Medano Beach.

Mango Beach Bar and Grill and the Office are the best place for margaritas, food, and people watching. Mango has a two-for-one happy hour from 7 AM to 7 PM every day. From Medano Beach you have a great view of the rocky shore across and South of the marina. And you can see the Arch, or El Arco. I recommend a day excursion, approximately a one hour drive, to Todos Santos North of Cabo on the Pacific. Todos Santos is a small colonial town of artists and latter-day hippies. The streets are lined with small boutiques, a church, and a Spanish Plaza. Todos Santos is the home of the famous hotel California, and to visit it is to go back in time. Some call Todos Santos "el pueblo magico," the magical village.

There are 14 square blocks in the historic center of Todos Santos where art galleries abound. There are many restored historic buildings. Todos Santos is the home of the annual Festival de cine Todos Santos, a film festival. Also, there is a small history and culture museum.

For lunch in Todos Santos I suggest the Tequila Sunrise Bar and Grill in the center of town on Calle Juarez near hotel California.

In the winter months, I suggest going whale watching in Cabo San Lucas. That's when the whales migrate around Cabo and travel up into the sea of Cortez to mate. There are many options for whale watching tours. I recommend either Cabo Expeditions or Cabo Escape. They depart from the marina.

Cabo escape offers sunset and snorkeling cruises. They can be contacted by your hotel or at 624 105 0177. You can find them at caboescapetours.com.

Cabo expeditions is also known for its whale watching tours. They can be contacted at 624 143 2700 or caboexpeditions.com.mx. Fishing in Cabo San Lucas has been called the "sport fishing" capital of the world or "the Marlin capital of the world." It is at the tip of Baja where the land end. In Spanish it is called "Finnis Terra", or the end of the land. It is where the Pacific Ocean on the West converges with the sea of Cortez. Each ocean has different currents and water temperatures. The convergence forms a unique ecology, or feeding ground for the fish.

Contact Venture sports fishing Cabo San Lucas BCS MX info@venturecabofishing.com. They Specialize in fishing charters in either large, medium, and small charter boats. Prices range from 650 - 2500 USD. They also have a surf fishing at 120 USD, Most people that rooster fish when surf fishing. It is located between Hidalgo and Morelos near Hwy. 19 on Calle Alikan. A variety of fish are attracted to the Cape area. It makes for great fishing. It is a an unforgettable experience for the sport fishermen. Also, there is always a party at night in Cabo San Lucas, whether you can catch a fish or not. A trip to Cabo is an unforgettable travel experience.

Los Cabos, The main town in Cabo San Lucas, is called the "crown jewel of the Baja Peninsula." The popular Medano Beach is beautiful. There is world–class sport fishing, whale watching, snorkeling, and golf. Cabo is also known for its wild and crazy nightlife where one can party like a Rock star. There are many choices for activities. Cabo San Lucas is no longer just a sleepy fishing village. When you return home you will have a lifetime of memories. Enjoy!

13

The Corridor of Los Cabos and East Cape Baja BCS

"For my part, I travel not to go anywhere, but to go. I travel for travel's sake. The great affair is to move."

–Robert Louis Stevenson

The "corridor" is the highway connecting Cabo San José along the coast to Cabo San Lucas. The distance is about 20 miles. It is a scenic ride connecting the sea of Cortez to the Pacific. It ends at Finnis Terra, or Los Arcos, and is the "end of the land". It is great for fishing, and golf. Many golf courses have been built along this route.

Hernan Cortes explored the area and wrote about it in the late 1500s and early 1600s. They gave it the name of California. Later the Jesuits built missions, and wrote about their discoveries. Of course, the indigenous natives were the first to settle there. William Walker, from Tennessee in the USA, was next to arrive on the scene, he was an eccentric who wanted to rule his own country. Baja was his first attempt to have his own country.

In 1853, Walker and his small group of soldiers, arrived in La Paz. They deposed the governor and raised their own flag. The Mexican army opposed and walker fled. He was captured crossing the border and was tried and sentenced to jail in the US. The US did not support his actions. Later he was shot and killed in Honduras after trying to form a country in Central America.

The growth of tourism in the modern era occurred in the 1950s. This was the era of the fly-ins resorts using single engine airplanes. Many hotels built their own air strips to attract fishermen and tourists. The idea caught on, especially by Hollywood notables, Baja BCS was now on the map! Los Cabo's became the playground of John Wayne, Bing Crosby, Phil Harris, Dezi and Lucy Arnez. It was becoming the place to see and be seen.

The fly-ins played an important role in the development of Baja. The one and only Hotel Palmilla is located a few miles south of Cabo San Jose. It first opened in 1956. The original owners were Rod Rodriguez and Bud Parr. Rodriguez was the son of a Mexican president. He lived the life of a rich playboy. Parr had served in the USA intelligence in world war II. The hotel had its own fly-ins landing strip. There is also a Jack Nicklaus golf course. The hotel became popular with the rich and famous. Today it has gone through a renovation and is still the best in luxury. How to contact the Palmilla telephone 1 877 999 0680 or visit www.oneandonlypalmillaresorts. com. The landscaping is fascinating. It is located by the sea of Cortez and has beachfront access. Airport transfers are included. The construction of the trans-peninsular highway in 1970 caused the hotel to become more popular than ever before. Nightly rates started at 624USD. The one and only Pamilla is located off the trans-peninsular highway at KM 27 near Punta Pamilla and San Jose.

In the 1960s Parr built the hotel Cabo San Lucas. Many celebrities stayed here. Cabo was now on the tourists map for certain. Cary grant was a frequent visitor. In Todos Santos the hotel California opened in 1950. Today it has been renovated by a Canadian couple John and Debbie Stewart. Its legacy lives in the song "Hotel California" by the Eagles in 1976. Fly-ins in Baja are no longer needed. Now there is an international, SJD.

In 1997 the new modern Los Cabos International opened. Commercial airline connections are now available. The airport (SJD) is located on the corridor door between San Jose and Cabo San Lucas. There is a small airfield in Cabo San Lucas for private planes. It is located north of the city.

San Jose del Cabo. San Jose was founded as a mission town in the 18th century. It has the look and feel of colonial Mexico. There are numerous small shops. The Cathedral is the focal point of the historic town. Many art galleries can be found in San Jose. San Jose Cabo Hotels.

Cabo del sol This is an important hotel 40USD ideal for a family. Includes a kitchen, free Wi-Fi and TV sleeps three. Surf Hostel Cabo exit 29KM trans-peninsular highway 23400 San José BCS. Dorm bedrooms 125USD per bed. Share bath. Free Wi-Fi and TV. Beachfront location. For the budget minded traveler and surfer. Santa Maria hotel 94USD near beach. Pool, AC, TV and Wi-Fi.

Paseo Los Cabo's 140 club de golf 23467 San Jose. Great location.

Hotel Colli 55USD Zaragoza and doblado Telephone number +624 142 0725 refurbished. Small clean rooms, AC, downtown location close to shopping and Cathedral budget class. Los Barriles drive North on Highway 19, or the peninsular highway to reach Los Barriles on the sea of Cortez. It is a laid back fishing village. A place to get away from the frantic activity of Cabo San Lucas.

The Sea of Cortez is said to be the wind surfing capital. Jacques Cousteau called the sea of Cortez "the aquarium of the world." Fishing is excellent. Also there is a whale watching. Los Barriles Hotel, 62USD, just a short walk to the beach and the kite boarding school. Large rooms and comfortable beds, free Wi-Fi. Calle 20 de Noviembre 50 23330 Los Barriles BCS. Hotel Palmas de Cortez 131USD located on the beach. Fishing reservations available. Spa, swim up bar, AC, fishing charters, good food and service four stars. You will Ave 20 De Noviembre #2 Los Barriles 23330 BCS. Los Barriles restaurants Tio Pablos the great burgers, shrimp, pizza. Moderate prices, TV sports. Happy hour for 4-6 PM. Specials every night example prime rib.

Caleb's Café best for breakfast and lunch. Prices reasonable. Middle of town. Omelettes and strawberry pancakes. El Greco Beach Club Mexican food, fish and tacos. Can't go wrong. Travel north from Los Barriles and you come to Loreto. It was founded by the Spanish in the 17th century and is known for its mission, our lady of Loreto. It was the capital for Baja 132 years. Today, it is a mecca for fishermen. The hotel oasis can arrange fishing and whale watching.

Cave paintings in Baja are located near Loreto in the mountain region of Sierra de San Francisco. There are some hundred prehistoric cave paintings discovered in Baja by anthropologists. The indigenous artists painted birds, turtles, fish and deer on the cave walls. Only a government official guide can escort the tourists to see them. They are protected by UNESCO. The cave paintings date back 1500 years. La Paz, next to the sea of Cortez, is rich in history with the old world charm, but embracing the modern culture.

The Malecon is the focal point of the city. It has many fine restaurants. There is the beach and the marina. Fishing is popular. There is scuba diving, and whale watching. Something for everybody. La Paz is the Spanish word for "The Peace." The people seem to be at peace, and very friendly.

La Paz Hotels

La Paz Hotels Hotel Perla 54USD TV, Wi-Fi, fans, AC. Great location on Malecon water front. Alvaro Obrego 1570 Centro 23000. Well-known historic hotel. Near the anthropology Museum. Pool, TV, Wi-Fi, and AC. One La Paz Hotel 44USD Nicolas Bravo 590 ESQ Ignacio La Paz 23000. Historical district near history Museum. Hotel Marina del Sol 48USD Wi-Fi, AC, bath and great view. La Paz Centro 10 minutes #1 Marina Fidepaz BCS.

Seven Crown La Paz Hotel 55USD near Malecon. La

Paz restaurants Buffalo BBQ madero1145 US20 for BBQ steaks and burgers. Fish of the day. Popular with locals and tourists.

Las TresVirgenes, Madero1130, has elegant seafood risotto, sea snails, and tuna. Upscale dining. It is also. taco and fish restaurant. A local favorite. A good value.

Marques Aves de Leon and heroes Independence. Tailhunters Cantina. Mexican seafood not expensive. Avenida Alvaro Obregon 755, 23020 La Paz BCS. Great view. Mango margaritas. Will cook your fish. But has fish of the day. Great ceviche. Reasonable prices and good service.

The Rustico. "Best restaurant in La Paz." Revolution de 1910, Pueblo Nuevo 23004 La Paz BCS. Known for its wood fire pizza. Most people prefer to dine outside on the patio in the Italian garden. Other favorites are pasta pesto, carpaccio's, salads, lobster ravioli and bistec ranchero. Owned and managed by an Italian couple from Tuscany. The chef is Italian.

The Dock is well known for its American breakfast. Also, seafood, salads, and burgers. Located in the marina with great views. Reasonable prices. Service may vary. Located at Topete 3040 Barrio Manglito 230604.

14

Health and Safety in Mexico

"Twenty years from now you will be more disappointed by the things you didn't do than by the ones you did do."

— Mark Twain

Health and Safety. Today there are people who are afraid to travel in Mexico because of the news reporting in the USA and elsewhere. I have been traveling to Mexico for twenty years with no encounters or problems. Once I was treated in a hospital in Cabo with excellent medical care. I have no reservations about my travel in Mexico, but I do not do drugs and I mind my own business. I keep a low profile. I am not the loud ugly Norte Americano.

The drug cartels are found mostly in the border cities of Juarez or Tijuana. The problems occur mostly with the confrontation with law enforcement, and people who deal in the drug trade. Most people do not encounter any problems. When driving in Mexico at night it is best to exercise caution. Try to pull over at night and stay at a hotel, or an organized camp. It is better to be safe than sorry. Don't walk down dark streets, or alleys late at night, especially if you have had a few drinks.

The Mexican drug cartels market most of their drugs in the USA. They are the suppliers. It is because the demand for drugs is insatiable. The US has followed an interdiction strategy, and has tried to work with various Mexican presidents to prevent the production and shipment of drugs into the USA. In some ways, this has caused the cartels to become more competitive with each other resulting in increased violence and warfare. Regardless, the policy of the USA is to encourage the Mexican government to increase their anti-drug efforts. The cartels combat these efforts by using their money for bribery and corruption. It is a vicious circle. Don't get involved in the drug trade.

Mexican drug smugglers used drones recently to smuggle heroin into the USA. The weight was too much and the drone crashed. Expect drones will be used more often. Drug dealers also use tunnels. One was discovered near San Diego. El Chapo was arrested in 2016. He was the world's most wanted drug Lord in Mexico. President Pena Nieto of Mexico cannot afford the embarrassment when El Chapo escaped. This may be the end for El Chapo. Crime is a fact of life no matter where you are, even in the USA. Don't make yourself a target of crime. Always be aware of your surroundings. Be vigilant. Do not wear expensive jewelry, wear only an old cheap watch. Do not have a camera around your neck and a guidebook, or a map in your hand. Put your wallet in your front pocket.

Leave your passport in your room, or hotel safe. Carry

only the cash you need, or use a money belt. Leave some of your credit cards and money in the hotel room or safe. Try to blend in as much as possible. Do not bring attention to yourself. Consume less alcohol. Travel with a friend when possible. Make copies of all documents.

Center for disease control and prevention, or CDC, Atlanta, GA USA. The CDC recommends certain vaccines and medications for travel to Mexico. A person should visit their doctor or travel clinic 4 to 6 weeks before travel. Make sure you are up to date on your vaccines and keep your vaccine papers with your passport for evidence.

Typhoid- you can get typhoid by consuming contaminated food or water. This is important if you are an adventure traveler, or you are visiting in rural areas of smaller cities.

Hepatitis A - this shot protects you against contaminated food or water in Mexico.

Rabies - this is not a major risk in Mexico. Dogs are everywhere in the streets. Avoid petting animals.

Routine vaccinations - many travel clinics recommend a polio update. Tetanus and a flu shot are also a good idea. On my last trip I accidentally cut my arm, luckily I had a tetanus booster before traveling.

Hepatitis B - hepatitis B can be contracted by way of sexual contact, dirty needles, blood transfusion, for a tattoo or piercing.

Malaria - avoid mosquitoes to prevent bites. Use a sleeping net. Wear long pants, and long sleeve shirts. Use a bug spray with DEET. Malaria is rare in Mexico. But your doctor, or travel clinic can prescribe a malaria pill for you. Keep taking the pill until you finish the prescription. I have never taken malaria pills for Mexico. Only when I go to Africa.

Diarrhea - some people call it traveler's diarrhea, others call it "Montezuma's revenge." Regardless it can occur when consuming uncooked food, or water or beverage that is unpurified. The famous slogan "if you cannot peel it do not eat it." So, eat and drink safely. Diarrhea occurs when the bowel or stools, are loose and watery. It typically lasts three days. Dehydration occurs because there is something in the bowel which draws water from the body. More than likely the body has an infection, or bacteria. Often in Third World countries there are open sewers, unpurified hydrate water, food improperly washed or prepared, or simply a fly which lands on your food and spreads a bacteria. I have had episodes of diarrhea when I had to lay in bed for two or three days. I could not eat, and I was miserable. You can just let it run its course, or treated with over-the-counter Pepto-Bismol or Imodium A/D. Consume as much water as possible, or Gatorade to restore the electrolyte. Snack on crackers, bananas or toast. If it is bloody diarrhea go to a doctor or clinic such as St. Luke's in Todos Santos. My doctor gives me some antibiotics when I travel. The antibiotics can get to the source of the bacteria and knock it out. The Imodium can stabilize the bowel system. The travel with stress, and change of environment, along with new foods can cause "travel diarrhea." Look to see if your urine is clear, or not. Your goal is to have clear urine. Stay hydrated! Cloudy urine means you are not drinking enough water. This way you can overcome "Montezuma's revenge."

DVT

Deep vein thrombosis (DVT) I have suffered from the DVT and have been treated for this. If not treated it can be deadly. This usually occurs when seated in cramped quarters over a long period of time with dehydration, and lack of exercise. It occurs when a blood clot forms, or blood pools in the deep veins of the leg. The dangers if not treated the blood clot can break off and flows up to the lungs. This can cause death. My story is that when I returned home from a nine-hour airline economy seat I felt like I had a muscle pulled in my left leg. Eventually, thank God, I called my doctor and describe the problem. He advised me to go to the hospital immediately. He would be waiting for me. I was treated with vitamins,elevated leg and blood thinners. I was in the hospital for seven days. But his quick advice saved my life. So don't delay if you need treatment. You may need to stay on blood thinners for six months.

Hangovers affect many tourists, especially younger people, often because of overindulge in alcohol consumption in Mexico. The beer, and the tequila flows freely, especially when on vacation and there is a party atmosphere. The most common symptoms of a hangover are; dehydration, nausea, fatigue, and headache. Treatment of the hangover is to drink water to hydrate, or Gatorade to replace electrolytes. Eat some food. "The hair of the dog" is only a temporary cure. Prevention should be considered in the future. Do not drink too quickly, or guzzle. Drink water when you can when you consume alcohol. Eat some food. Stay with the same type of drink as you started with.

Sunburn, many tourists travel to Mexico because of the abundance of sunshine and warm climate. Also, diving and fishing are excellent. Many people overdo their activities in the sunshine which results in sunburn. Always wear a hat, and a top shirt as a shield from the sun. It is best to use a sun block of 35 – 50 SPE sunscreen. When snorkeling remember to put sunscreen on the back of your legs and wear a T-shirt in the water.

Medical care healthcare in Mexico is very good, and in many places it is excellent. Most doctors and dentists in Mexico received at least part of their medical training in the USA. Cost of healthcare in Mexico is generally half or less of what you might expect to pay in the USA. Drugs usually are 50% less, and are available without a prescription. St. Luke's is an emergency clinic open 24 hours in Todos Santos. English is spoken in St. Luke's. They offer consultation without a doctor, laboratory work, and hospitalization. The address is H. Colegio Militar at Col. El Centro Todos Santos BCS telephone number 612 145 0600. They can arrange both air and ground transportation.

St. Luke's accepts both national and international insurance. They also take Visa and MasterCard. The email is hertor@saintlukesclinic.com.

Ameri-Med Hospital is in Cabo San Lucas, Boulevard Lazaro Carderas at El Medano paseo marina and Pesador telephone number 624 105 8500. It is a short walk from El Centro just as you pass by the new shopping mall. The staff is bilingual and is open 24 hours. It is an American type Hospital in Mexico specializing in the care of international travelers. They have traditional practitioners, and doctors who can do stitches. Email rrojas@amerimed-hospitals.com.

On my recent visit to Cabo I needed medical care since I had tripped on an uneven sidewalk at night and had a cut on my left arm. The Ameri-med gave me a prompt and courteous service. The doctor was well trained. He and his intern drained my wound, and used antibiotics completely over the wound. He bandaged the wound, and prescribed antibiotics. I traveled home the next day to Atlanta. My doctor in Atlanta commented the doctor in Mexico had done a great job with proper treatment.

I paid with my American Express in Mexico, and applied for and received a refund from my USA insurance company. I was pleased with the quality of service of Ameri-med. Hotels can advise and recommend private physicians.

But, if you need a house call in Cabo, I called Dr. James McAllister who is a board-certified physician who makes house calls, His telephone number 044 624 141 6176. In La Paz, the Salvatierra Hospital is recommended for tourist's healthcare. It is near the intersection of Forjedores and Coloso. Many say it is the best hospital in Baja especially for cardiac cases.

Travel insurance medical travel insurance will help protect you from financial ruin if you have an emergency and need medical care in another country. You don't want your savings wiped out because of an accident overseas. Also, you may need to be airlifted back to your home country.

Why travel insurance?

1. your passport was lost or was stolen?
2. your baggage was lost?
3. you need medical treatment for an emergency?
4. you have an accident or just turned your ankle?
5. Your cruise line or travel agency goes bankrupt.
6. There is a terrorist incident?
7. You lose your money or travel checks?
8. A hurricane occurs while on vacation and need to evacuate the trip without interruption?
9. Emergency evacuation especially if you are in a remote country or mountain climbing?
10. Trip cancellation interrupted, or delayed?

"Insure my trip" is a quick web site to use when you are shopping for travel insurance and need to compare various policies to meet your needs. The Representatives do not receive a sales commission. They find the best plan for your trip. Then it is your choice. The reps will stay on the phone with you if it takes to satisfy your various policy needs. Your questions will be answered so that you can find the best plan for your trip needs. They are in Rhode Island USA Telephone number 1-800-487-4722 or email Customercare@insuremytrip.com.

Travel guard travel insurance is one of my favorites and a leading provider of travel insurance plans and assistance, just Telephone 1-800-826-4919.

Allianz global assistance has a unique purchase plan which allows you to review a period of your contract. If for any reason, you wish to cancel your plan during the review. Your premium will be refunded if you have not filed a claim Telephone number 1-866-884-3556. Allianz, po box 71533, Richmond VA 23286-4684.

World nomads is a leading provider of international travel insurance. Located in Sydney Australia. Telephone number 1-800-611-210 and a free call from Australia, or. Telephone number 612 8263 0470 Email assist@worldnomads.com/travelinsurance. They are backed up by Lloyds and Bupa global travel, underwriters. They are popular and well trusted. It just makes good sense to cover yourself with travel insurance. USA Department of state travel warnings and alerts are available from the US Department of State.

Advice on how to find a US embassy or consulate overseas if the passport is lost, or you go to jail. Email travel.state.gov or USA.GOV telephone number 1-877-487-2778.

Contact the USA Department of State for traveler's problems internationally. STEP is a free service, or US citizens traveling overseas. Enrollment is for emergencies abroad. The nearest US Embassy or Consulate is notified about your trip. Another website to check regarding your health for travelers and vaccinations is traveler vaccines. com. You need to visit their website before you travel to foreign countries. You will learn about diseases you may encounter and immunizations that might need that might be appropriate. Always do your homework, and be aware of your surroundings. It is good to know your options if there is an emergency. Travel safe and enjoy.

15

Final words why I travel?

Why I travel "Man cannot discover new oceans unless he has the courage to lose sight of the shore"

-Andre Gide

Travel is my passion. My first major trip was to Mexico City, one of my favorite cities. I saw museums, colonial architecture, and the great pyramids to the Aztec sun and moon gods.

The travel "bug" got me, and continues today to motivate me to explore the world. My college studies of history, Geography, and languages have contributed to my motivation to travel. Later, after a trip to Québec city, I took my first trip to Europe. I was impressed by the museums, history, and architecture. Travel and learning became an obsession and would not let go. I was hooked forever on travel. Just give me an airline ticket, and I am happy. By this time I had received my Masters in history. Traveling and learning was a passion. Travel is a university. I learned to travel on a budget. If you can dream it you then you can do it. My greatest travel accomplishments was climbing Mount Kilimanjaro. I still love Africa, especially Kenya and Tanzania where I travel frequently.

I have traveled to all seven continents of the world. Antarctica was special to see. The polar bears of Canada in the Arctic made a lasting impression. Traveling the trans-Siberian Railroad from Beijing, and to Mongolia, and to Moscow ranks high on my list. A must see is the Hermitage in St. Petersburg Russia. I was in Berlin just after the wall came down in 1989. How exhilarating! I shall never forget. I have many pieces of the wall at home. Travel is my goal in life.

But it almost came to an end in 2009 while traveling to Patagonia Chile in the winter. While hiking I slipped on ice and had a severe break of my right ankle. It took two years and six operations to save my ankle. Plus rehab. My ankle will never be normal. I had to retire from my job because I walk with a cane. I continue to travel, but I will no longer be climbing mountains. My motto is "Just go"!!

Top 10 reasons why I travel?

1) Travel opens your eyes to larger views of world cultures?
2) Learn a new language, and enjoy your new culture?
3) Adventure and excitement. For the fun of it.
4) Education travel is a university where you learn firsthand what you cannot learn in a classroom. Travel is an education.

5) Make a dream come true. See the Egyptian pyramids and Taj Mahal in India.

6) Stories to tell for the rest of your life. Or write travel books.

7) New and exotic foods such as grilled grasshoppers in Zimbabwe?

8) To prove yourself you can. You can climb Mount Kilimanjaro, or the Himalayas in Nepal. It is a challenge and a sense of accomplishment.

9) See the environment firsthand. See the monkeys and the birds of Costa Rica or the lion, and cheetah in Tanzania and Kenya. The polar bears of the Arctic. The immigrating whales off Baja Mexico. Turtle release in Todos Santos?

10) To find yourself. Just as the Beatles traveled to India. Find the meaning in your life? Everyone has a reason to travel. You have seen my reasons for travel. I will continue to travel. Just go! Enjoy life! "pura vida!"

"It's a wonderful world."

Louis Armstrong
Please remember to
take care of our planet.

"If you do not have a story to tell then you have never traveled."

–John P. Cross, Author.

Appendix 1

Packing check list / Travel check list

"When preparing to travel, layout all your clothes and all your money. Then take half the clothes and twice the money."

                                        –Susan Heller

Items to pack

- Alarm clock, Camera and memory card/film
- Electrical adapters and converters
- Mini First Aid kit
- Soap and shampoo
- Sunscreen and Sunglasses
- Toiletries
- Prescriptions
- Toilet paper
- Passport & Visa
- Mini detergent packs
- Clothes line and Sink stopper
- Face Cloth
- Airline tickets and Vaccination Certificate

- Swimsuit Parka, and Coat
- Anti-bacterial wipes/Hand Sanitizer/ Diarrhea pills
- Bug spray/insect repellent Pen & notebook
- Flashlight/ torch /sewing kit
- Plastic Bags Credit cards & ATM card
- Calculator and Money belt
- Umbrella Poncho/raincoat
- Flip flops/ Mobile phone/International SIM
- Luggage locks
- Copy of up to date passport
- Travel Insurance

This packing check list is only a suggestion. It depends where you are going, and the climate. Also, there are cultural differences in what you wear, especially for women. A long skirt instead of shorts or long pants, the famous "little black dress" is universal. Men should have long pants as well as shorts. A light sweater, and jacket may be needed. Cold climate requires thermal underwear.

Appendix 2

Computer Apps: The New World of the mobile device in travel

"Getting information off the internet is like taking a drink from a fire hydrant."

 –Michell Kapoor

Apps have become popular in the travel world today. No discussion is complete without the use of apps. They can save you time and money. Most are free. I will only attempt to cover the most important ones for travel today. Here is a list of apps to help you: plan

Kayak – Kayak makes it possible for you to search for the best airfare by comparing different airline prices for a given date.

Booking.com – Is an online hotel reservation website owned by

Priceline. They guarantee the lowest priced rooms. The room fee is not charged until you check into the room.

Trivago – is the world's largest hotel metasearch, in other words, it searches all hotel sites and combines them for easy search of what you are looking for. It can search by price.

Trip advisor – it is a travel website based upon user travel locations such as hotels, restaurants, and tourist attractions. Visitors reviews are its trademark.

XE Currency app for I phone – Allows you to convert every currency and gives you exchange rates and historical data. It is the most downloaded foreign exchange app. There are free daily currency updates.

The weather channel app – Hour by hour forecasts with radar maps, can monitor hurricanes worldwide.

Google Translate – Has a unique mode. Simply open the mobile device while two people are speaking a language. The words will be translated instantly. Day to day words are translated right away. It can translate a menu or a road sign.

Google Maps – Gives road turn by turn directions. It will identify restaurants, and tourist attractions along the way. Offers the traveler a wealth of roadside information as you travel.

Tingo – an app to help the traveler find a hotel by location and price.

Seat Guru – This finds you the best seats on the plane. You can select the seat with the most leg room. It also gives you flight status updates.

Oanda –Currency conversion up to date exchange rates for you on your travels. It provides a free cheat sheet and print a copy for your wallet. Daily rates from your mobile device. Never over pay again.

Hotels Tonight – if you need a room ASAP or tonight their app will give you options quickly. Book as late as 2AM.

Trip it – This app will create your master itinerary. You become your own travel agent. It can find the best seats on the plane. Includes directions, maps, and weather.

As you can see, there are almost unlimited Travel app sites. They will aid you in finding the best travel deals. A well-stocked mobile device is as essential as a passport. There are almost too many choices available.

Appendix 3

Spanish Travel Dictionary/ Basic Spanish for the Tourist

"If you talk to a man in a language he understands, that goes to his head. If you talk to him in his own language, that goes to his heart."

–Nelson Mandela

The best way to learn Spanish, or any language is to ask questions. Your understanding of a language and cultural awareness goes a long way in making friends and negotiating the price of a souvenir, or artifact. Just try. Don't be afraid. Your efforts will be appreciated. Spanish is the second most popular language in the world, after English. Spanish is the official language in thirty world countries.

COGNATES

Cognates makes it easier to learn Spanish. Congnates are words in two languages that have a similar meaning. Spelling, and pronunciation. Spanish has many cognates which relate to English words. Some examples are accidente or accident, and decider, or decide. Similar words in Spanish and English make learning and retention faster.

GREETINGS

SI --- YES
NO---NO
HOLA---HELLO
ADIOS---GOODBYE
POR FAVOR---PLEASE
GRACIAS---THANK YOU
PERDON--- THANK YOU OR PARDON ME
BUENOS DIAS--- GOOD MORNING
BUENAS TARDES--- GOOD AFTERNOON
BUENAS NOCHES--- GOOD NIGHT

QUESTIONS

QUE TAL--- WHAT'S UP?
COMO ESTAS—HOW ARE YOU?
COMO TE LLAMAS--- WHATS YOUR NAME?
QUE AHORAS--- WHAT TIME IS IT?
DONDE ESTA--- WHERE IS
BANO--- BATHROOM

POR QUE--- WHY?
QUANTO--- HOW MUCH?
BARATO--- CHEAPER
UNA MAS--- ONE MORE
CERVEZA--- BEER
VINO---WINE
CAUNTO CUESTA--- HOW MUCH PRICE?

MENU AND QUESTIONS

PESCADO--- FISH
CAMARON--- SHRIMP
POLLO---CHICKEN
CARNE DE VACA--- BEEF
CERDO--- PORK
AUTO BUS--- BUS
COLECTIVO--- SHARE A VAN
DE NADA--- WELCOME
GRACIAS--- THANK YOU
POR FAVOR--- PLEASE
MI NOMBRE ES--- MY NAME IS?
COMIDA--- TO EAT OR MEALS
COMOTELLAMAR—WHAT IS YOUR NAME?
QUIERO--- I WANT
LA CARTA--- MENU
EL DESAYUNO--- BREAKFAST
ALMUERZO -- LUCH
CENA--- DINNER
BUENO--- GOOD
LA QUENTA--- CHECK, HOW MUCH?
BEBIDA--- TO DRINK

PHRASES

PURA VIDA--- GREETINGS, LIFE IS GOOD, ENJOY. HOW IS IT GOING? (COSTA RICA)
CON MUCHO GUSTO- IT HAS BEEN MY PLEASURE
CHAO- GOODBYE

You may decide that you need a Spanish tutor before you travel to learn enough basic vocabulary and phrases and to ask questions. Your trip will be more meaningful if you do. Learn a New language, and enjoy a new culture and your trip.

Rosetta Stone language courses is an excellent way to learn a second language. Contact www.rosettastonestone.com. They offer CD'S and a mobile app. You can hear the native accents as well

A reference-Collins, Spanish concise Dictionary, 3rd ed. Harper Collins, NYC USA,2006

Another way to study a language is to use Babbel, which includes fourteen languages. Access Babbel at www.babbel.com. Babble has apps which are compatible with the iPhone, tablet, and the pc. All free of charge. You can use it to translate on the go, or home. It is easy and fun to use. Babbel is similar to playing a computer game.

Appendix 4

Bibliography

Aitchison, The Desert Islands of Mexico Sea of Cortez, U Arizona press Tucson, Arizona 2010

Beezley and Meyer, The oxford history of Mexico. Oxford U 2010 NYC, NY USA

Brenner, the wind that swept Mexico: The history of the Mexican Revolution of 1910-1942, University of Texas press, Austin, Texas 3rd printing 1984

Burkholder & Johnson Colonial Latin America 2nd Edition Oxford u press NYC, NY USA 1994Burton, The History of Mexico. Macmillan NYC, NY USA 2000

Camp, Mexico: What Everyone Needs to know. Oxford U. Press NYC, NY USA 2011

Crosby, the cave paintings of Baja California, Discovering the great murals of an unknown people, 1975 Sunbelt publications San Diego, California

Collins, Spanish concise Dictionary, 3rd ed. Harper Collins, NYC USA, 2006

Cruch and Cruch, Traveler's guide to camping Mexico's Baja with your RV or tent Traveler's guide USA 2012.

Delgado, Explorer's guide to Los Cabos and Baja California sur: A great destination The Country Mans press Woodstock, Vermont USA 2011,

Eder, Whales and other Marine Mammals of California and Baja. Lone Pine press, California USA 2002

Emmons, The book of tequila: A complete guide. Open Court publication company USA 1997

Franz, The peoples guide to Mexico revised 1988. John Muir publications Santa Fe, NM U.S.A

Fodor's Los Cabos with Todos Santos and La Paz 2nd edition NYC USA 2013

Goth-Iton, Los Cabos including La Paz and Todos Santos Avalon travel. Moon books Berkley, CA USA 2013

Gatch, Tom, hooked on Baja Where and how to fish Mexico's legendary waters. 2009 country man press NYC, NY USA

Thomas, The conquest of Mexico. Pimlico Random house London 2004.

Hamilton, Frommer's Los Cabos and Baja, John Wiley and Sons Inc. Hoboken, NJ USA 2012

Hagus, Treasures of Todos Santos. Mill city press, Minneapolis, MN USA 2007.

Jones, Gray Whales: my twenty years of discovery. Create spam publishing, Arizona 2012

Mad Coyote Joe, A gringo guide to authentic Mexican cooking Northland publications, Flagstaff, Arizona USA 2001

Meade, Living abroad in Mexico. Moon books, Avalon press Berkley, CA USA 2005

Miller, Mexico A History U. Oklahoma press. Norman, OK USA 1985.

National Geographic Maps, Baja California BCS Mexico, Washington, DC USA 2014

Nieman, Greg, Baja legends: The historic characters, events, and locations that put Baja California on the map. Sunbelt Cultural heritage books, USA 2014

Parise, Mike The surfers guide to Baja USA 2012

Peevers, Lonely planet. Baja California Lonely planet publishers Melbourne, Australia 2001

Peterson, The Baja adventure book Wilderness press USA 1999

Poniatowska, Las Soldaderas Women of the Mexican revolution. Cinco Puntas press 2006 El Paso, TX USA

Rebman, Baja California Plant Field Guide 3rd edition Sunbelt publications San Diego, CA USA 2012

Revolution of 1910 -1942, U Texas press Austin Texas 1984

Thetion, Legendary Hotel California. Todos Santos BCS Mexico. Todos Santos 2013

Thomson, Birding in Baja California Sur. Eco adventures Todos Santos MX 2014

Vaugham, The Eagles: An American band. Sterling press, USA 2010

Page, Mexico: Health and safety travel guide, 2nd edition Med to Go, LLC USA 2007.

Webb, The World Atlas of Beer Optopus Press London UK 2012

Wilbur, Birds of Baja California, U California press Berkley, California USA 1987

Wildeman, Welcome to Mexico Gringo, Amazon digital press USA 2014

Appendix 5

Budgeting: Definition of cost

Budget- How to save money. Less than fifty dollarsUSD.
Moderate- Mid-range 40-60 dollarsUSD
Expensive- More elaborate. 100 dollars or more USD

JOHN P. CROSS is the Author of JUST GO: A global guide to budget Travel, 2015 Iuniverse

"A journey of a thousand miles must begin with a single step."

-LAO TZU

This adventure travel book is the life experiences of the author where man meets the world. Mexico is his favorite. May you benefit from the author's experiences. Follow your dream. There is no limit to the beautiful travel memories you may accumulate in your lifetime of travel. "He who is outside his door already has the hardest part of his journey behind him."

Index

Y

Yoga Classes 12, 37

Z

Zapata 1, 2, 3, 54, 55

Printed in the United States
By Bookmasters